LIFE
SPEAKS

A JOURNEY TO RECOGNIZING DIVINE PROVIDENCE IN YOUR LIFE

LIFE SPEAKS

Tammy J. Carpenter

"To the only God our Savior, through Jesus Christ our Lord, be glory, majesty, dominion and authority, before all time and now and forever. Amen."
Jude 1:25

DEDICATION

◆ ◆ ◆

In memory of my mother, Willie L. Carpenter, and my sister, Pamela "Sista" Gibson. The strength and tenacity that you both displayed while God allowed you here with us inspires me to keep going and to LIVE! Forever Loved. Always Remembered.

For my nieces, Shintara, DaLinda, Shonta, and Katrice; my goddaughter, Gabrielle and my enLife ladies, may my journey inspire you to recognize God in every phase of your life and believe Him above and beyond what you see and feel.

CONTENTS

FOREWORD

◆   ◆   ◆

One of the most rewarding things as a leader is to watch a mentee bloom. Ms. Tammy Carpenter is not only blooming, but she's developing a beautiful garden for all to see and to pick from. This book, *Life Speaks*, is her garden and in it is something for everyone.

You simply have to read and "pick" which part most impacts your life. You need to pick which part most declares to you how loudly your life has been speaking to you and trying desperately to draw you into the right direction. King Solomon tells us that Wisdom is crying in the streets, and I have found this to be true. To express her love for you, Wisdom has now recruited the pen of Tammy Carpenter to show you just how your life has been sending you messages all along, hoping to tweak your journey so that you can land in a place of righteousness and reach your expected end.

She is not only crying in the streets but she customizes a message to you that will explain the ebbs and flows of your life. She's trying to make you understand the meaning of your past so that you can, with more confidence, embrace a masterfully designed future that God has already prepared for you. In short, your life is working in concert with God to get you to your expected end.

So, join me as we walk through this garden that is revealed in the pages of this book and pick out the flowers that contain the fruit you've been missing. There are answers here for you. Remember, the diligent are guaranteed to find God and God is hidden throughout the pages of this book.

To quote King Solomon again, he tells us that, *"It is the glory of God to conceal a matter but it is the glory of kings to search out a matter." (Proverbs 25:2)* As you read this book, become the king of YOUR life who is on the scavenger hunt to find answers to what's still unfolding. Those answers are hidden in the pages of *Life Speaks*. Embrace them. Grow from them. Teach them. Much love.

Pastor Wendell Jones, Senior Pastor
Changing Your Mind Ministries – Greenville, SC

ACKNOWLEDGMENTS

◆ ——— ◆ ——— ◆

I am so fortunate to have an abundance of love and support! I know when mentioning names, I risk overlooking someone, so I apologize in advance!

My brothers, *Stan*, *Rick* and *Anthony*, my sisters in love, *Ferries*, *Florida* and *Sherry* and all of my nephews, nieces, great-nephews and great nieces, I love you guys!! We've suffered loss, but we're still laughing, loving and living. There is nothing like family! Much love to my *Gray & Oxner* family.

Pastor Wendell Jones, Lady Nita Jones thank you for saying "yes" to God and for making complacency uncomfortable. I'm getting my life! To the *Changing Your Mind Ministries family*, I started trying to list individual names, but there are too many to list. Your love, prayers and support enriches my life in so many ways. I've gained some lifelong family and friends and my heart delights in the gift of you.

To my *Gabrielle* – You are an answered prayer. I hope you know how proud I am of you and how grateful I am to be in your life. You are so beautiful to me!

My closest sister-friends (friendsters), *Trimeka, Christina, Rai Gai, Panora, Marthalene, Stephanie, Kendra* and *Charlene*. You ladies each have a special place in my life and in my heart. I'm ever grateful for your strength, love, consistency and years of friendship and sisterhood.

Bishop B. F. Johnny – You've made a permanent impression in my life. God knew and I'm grateful. Love you always.

Dr. Katrina Spigner - Thank you for boldly living and speaking your truth. You have inspired me and continue to inspire so many to release their voice.

Tamika "Ink Pen Diva" Sims - Your expertise and professionalism is incomparable. Thank you for coaching me through this writing process and not letting me quit the many times I wanted to.

Tanika Dillard - Thank you for penning your own story in such a captivating way and for nudging, encouraging and helping me see this to the end.

To *every young lady that I have met and will meet through enLife*, you are an intricate part of my journey and you are a constant reminder of God's love for me and His purpose for my life. Thank you for being you!

There are some people that have been a part of my life for many years and some entered in recent years and they fall in one of these categories: you are extended family, you are a repetitive source of encouragement, or you have proven to be a friend.

Helen Martin   *Demetral Butler*
Mike & Karen Jones   *Dr. T. Haulcy Thomas*
The Goodson Family   *Desmond & Valerie Thomas*
The Curry Family   *Quisha Dreher*
Pastor C. Prioleau   *Rev. Adrian & Nicole Bowens*
Leon Timbo   *& Family*

I can't name everyone but if you're reading this, I'm grateful for you and thank you for your support!

INTRODUCTION

◆   ◆   ◆

We all have a picture of how we think our life will turn out. We have childhood dreams of our ideal life. For me, I desired success. I loved seeing women leaders on magazine covers looking polished in their business suits. I imagined gracing the cover of a magazine one day. The blueprint for how this success would come was uncertain to me. Though not certain how, I still desired success. In the fifth grade, I wrote a poem titled, 'Being Me.'

Being Me
I meet different people along the way,
That show me the light each and every day.
When they were young, they did their best,
To make it these days and be a success.
They're on the right track, they've planted the right seeds,
They have all that they want and all that they need.
They live their lives right, they keep themselves straight,
They have wisdom, confidence and they know how to wait.
I'd like to be like them, and others that I see,
But I can get my success by just Being Me.

Success in life comes packaged with challenges. When looking at life and considering childhood dreams, you may end up on an unexpected path, yet still feel that you are right where you're supposed to be. As a young adult, my life collided with what I thought was my destiny. Everything within me agreed, and before I understood what mentoring was, I followed closely, took notes and left comfort zones.

You will discover in these pages the growth, challenges and transitions I experienced during my young adult years. I was content and settled with what I believed was the course of my life but in the midst of sudden and major changes, I landed in a mental and emotional whirlwind. While fighting to stay where I thought I was supposed to be, things fell apart resulting in a major transition in my life. I relied on the consistency of my faith and family though unexpected events continued to shake my foundation. Eventually, my present became uncertain and my future was unknown.

Life has many unexpected twists and turns, but there is beauty beyond those moments. As we walk with God, we learn that our steps are really ordered by Him. I had to release the reigns of my focus and desires in exchange for surrender and trusting God.

Through experience, I learned how personal God is. He truly is concerned about everything that concerns us and He orders our steps through the most difficult moments we face in life. I now know that even when He seems the furthest away, He is ever present, providing instructions for what's to come.

Each chapter shares personal events and lessons I learned from those moments. The LIFE Expression at the end of each chapter is a wisdom nugget followed by the Pause & Reflect; Pray & Listen section that provides you space to examine and apply the lesson to your life. *Embrace Your Journey!*

Note: Because these are true stories, names of individuals and locations involved have been changed to conceal identities.

"Now the Lord said to Abram, 'Go forth from your country, and from your relatives and from your father's house, to the land which I will show you'"
Genesis 12:1

━━━━━━━━━━◆━━━━━━◆━━━━━━◆━━━━━━━━━━

PURPOSED PROXIMITY

There are several occurrences in the Bible where God instructs individuals concerning their geographical location or position in relationships. A popular example is the story of Abram. God instructs Abram to leave his country and family with promises that He would make his name great and make him a great nation.

Relocating is about more than a change in scenery. Location matters. Environment matters. You never fully know what awaits you beyond change. Your certainty is in knowing that God has a plan for your life and that ALL things will work together for your good.

At the age of twenty five, deciding to move away from Greenville was major for me. I did not go off to college after high school. I stayed home, worked for a year and then attended a local technical school. I moved out of and back in to my mother's house a couple times, but remained close enough that it was easy to come back when I wanted or needed to.

> *Relocating is about more than a change in scenery.*

I didn't have a word from God or a promise of my name being great, but I felt strongly that this move was necessary for my life. Three years prior to making this decision, I met Evangelist Toni Dowdy. She was the keynote speaker at a conference in Greenville, and she preached three services that weekend. It was evident from the support and the crowd on the first night that she was well liked in the area. Though the little white building was standing room only, no one seemed to mind the crowded space. Impressive is an understatement when describing the effects this weekend had on me. I was captivated by how boldly and freely she declared the Word of God. I eagerly attended every service.

In the months and years to come, I continued to follow her ministry, Toni Dowdy Ministries (TDM). I attended various speaking engagements of hers and began to attend services held at her women's ministry, Leading Ladies Ministry (LLM). Regardless of where I had to travel to and what means I had to use to travel, including borrowed cars and the church van on an occasion, it became a priority and I made every effort to be at her engagements or events if I could. The response from people when Evangelist Dowdy preached was consistent. There was often packed out events and others that regularly traveled to follow her ministry.

It was about an hour and a half drive to LLM, and my trips became frequent, often several times per month. Women would travel from various cities in South Carolina to attend LLM events, so there were many that shared similar sentiments about Pastor Dowdy and her ministry. Though being a preacher and running a ministry was never a desire of mine, I was definitely intrigued by her level of success in ministry. Over time, I developed relationships with some of the ladies that were local and also a part of LLM. Minister Loman was one of them. She volunteered at LLM and would allow me to stay over at her house during some visits to alleviate me traveling so much. I had grown attached to this ministry and spending a lot of time of there.

Excerpt from my journal dated April 12, 1998:

The last weekend in March, Evangelist Dowdy was at Hope Fellowship. That was a year from the time I first heard her speak. I was able to speak with her briefly Sunday (3/29) morning before church. The admiration I have for her and LLM / TDM is different from what most people would think – the 'I want to be just like her when I grow up' admiration – yes, I do admire the way she so freely loves and gives of her time, treasure and talent as God requires, but I thank God that I've been taught to realize that she does what she does through Him alone. I'm also thankful that God has allowed me to better understand my feelings towards her. Although everything she does is for His glory and by His power, she chooses to be a willing vessel. Therefore, I long to be a blessing to her because she denies herself to bless others. Realizing that what God has done and is doing for her is for her, and what He has done and is doing in me is for me, my admiration & love does not desire to take from her, it's to give unto her.

Although LLM was not a church, my local pastor was concerned and felt that I couldn't have an allegiance to both the ministry and my local church. As a result, I slowly began to resign from the positions I held in church so I wouldn't have anything that would prohibit me from participating in TDM or LLM events. I admired Evangelist Dowdy's work in ministry as much as I admired her preaching. I had grown spiritually since connecting with her and desired to help her ministry in any way that I could. The more I made the trips, the more I felt that it was where I was supposed to be.

In August 2000 I packed up my blue Nissan Stanza hatchback with all of my belongings and relocated. Fortunately, I was able to transfer my job with my employer at the time. I had not planned or prepared financially in order to locate an apartment or establish a residence of my own once I moved, so I made arrangements to live with Minister Loman for a set monthly amount.

I arrived with an excitement for the unknown. I didn't know what was ahead for me, but I had no doubt that I was where God wanted me to be. Evangelist Dowdy traveled most weekends for speaking engagements. My initial plans did not include being a member of a local church so that I would have the freedom to support her. About a week before I moved, I received a call from Minister Loman to see if I would be interested in attending a meeting to discuss the formation of a church. Yes, Evangelist Dowdy was becoming a pastor.

The meeting was held about a day or so after I moved. There were ten of us in attendance. We discussed the name of the church, and the various positions and departments needed to establish a church. By the conclusion of the meeting, God's Grace International (GGI) was formed. I was member #10, and I was assigned the responsibility of Youth Leader since I held that position at my previous church. We started having weekly Bible study almost immediately and we held our first Sunday morning worship service a few months later. With the new church, ministry travel with TDM and regular events through LLM my schedule and life were filled with new experiences. It felt as if I stepped right into living the life God designed for me.

> *I stepped right into living the life God designed for me*

LIFE Expression:
A willingness to leap is necessary to make strides in life.

PAUSE & REFLECT. PRAY & LISTEN.

Consider a time that you were challenged to make changes geographically or relationally. How did that make you feel and how did you respond?

_____

_____

_____

_____

_____

_____

_____

_____

_____

_____

_____

_____

_____

_____

_____

"The Lord said, 'Behold, they are one people, and they all have the same language. And this is what they began to do, and now nothing which they purpose to do will be impossible for them.'"
Genesis 11:6

◆ ◆ ◆

COMMON UNITY

Let's look at a the definition of the word community:

community: *a group of men or women leading a common life according to a rule; a social, religious, occupational or other group sharing common characteristics or interests and perceived or perceiving itself as distinct in some respect from the larger society within which it exist.*

Communities are vital. Being a member of healthy communities is important to your personal development and growth. What's interesting about a community is that while it provides great strength to us, it also exposes our weaknesses. Whether it's among family or friends, during work or play, you will find yourself as part of many different communities. Members of certain communities are easily recognized because they share common looks, sounds or oftentimes both.

Learning is lifelong, and as a young adult woman there was still so much about life and relationships I had to learn. By

> *While it provides great strength to us, it also exposes our weaknesses*

relocating, I had unknowingly enrolled in a ripe boot camp.

7

Not only was I in a new city, but I was now part of a new community. There's a dynamic in close knit communities that's not often understood until you're in them. Before I moved, I remember having a brief conversation with one of the ladies that was part of the volunteer staff at Leading Ladies Ministry (LLM). I mentioned to her my desire to move was so that I could support the ministry more, and her reply was, *"You can support the ministry from Greenville with your checkbook."* Though it was an unexpected response, I didn't question her. We laughed it off and continued with other conversation. Shortly after moving, experiences helped me understand her comment.

Ms. Riley was also a volunteer at LLM. One Saturday afternoon she had to pick up Pastor Dowdy from the airport and Minister Loman was going to ride with her. Being new to the area, I asked Minister Loman if I could ride with them to give me an opportunity to see a little more of the city. After I asked to go, Minister Loman decided she was not going and told me to go ahead.

When I arrived to meet Ms. Riley, I greeted her and told her I was there to ride to the airport with her. She looked at me and said, *"You can't wear shorts to go pick up Pastor Dowdy from the airport!"* Puzzled and disappointed, I responded, *"Ok,"* and got back in my car. As I drove back to Minister Loman's house I thought, *Does she not realize it's summertime and it's HOT? What am I supposed to have on?* That was my first lesson in community standards.

Another lesson awaited me when I arrived back at Minister Loman's house. She knew that I was back too soon to have gone to the airport and she asked me why I did not go. I told her what transpired. Her response was, *"I could have told you that."* I thought, *Yea, then why didn't you?* She knew where I was going and saw me before I left her house. So really, why didn't she tell me? She then requested in a serious and firm tone that I not do that again. Seeing that my only action was requesting to accompany them, I understood that to mean don't impose on plans or ask to be a part of what I was not included in.

I retreated to the room I was renting in Minister Loman's home and reflected on what just happened. These both were eye opening encounters and my first mental notes of what not to wear and what not to do in the community. Though these were not pleasant experiences, they did not change my view about moving or being a part of this community.

As I became more acquainted with the women and families in the ministry, the common thread that unified them was evident. They were from different backgrounds, social classes and ethnicities, and many had experienced an almost crippling level of hurt in their past. It had been the love of God through the ministry of Pastor Dowdy over the years that helped them reach a place of recovery and restoration. Relationship with Pastor Dowdy appeared to be sacred to many. It's a natural response to be protective of that which has been our saving grace. We don't realize that sometimes when we strongly protect one thing or person, it causes detriment to another.

I lived with Minister Loman for about a year. When it was time for me to move, Pastor Dowdy secured a two bedroom apartment for me to live in, and she fully furnished the apartment. I shared the cost of the rent with the church because the apartment was made available to church members that traveled from other cities to attend services on the weekend. Pastor Dowdy frequently provided assistance to members of Leading Ladies Ministry (LLM) and God's Grace International (GGI).

> *Community began to shape my identity and standards*

Within a year another lady in the church needed a place to live. She moved in to the apartment with me to occupy the additional bedroom. That was another lesson in community. If a need was known, the community provided support.

I was in a new city, around new people, and I was constantly learning and changing as I adapted to the community. As a young adult woman, this new community began to shape my identity and standards. I learned the unspoken agreements, became shaped by the patterns and buried my silent rebellion. The longer you are a part of a community, you will become as they are. The more you spend time with others, you will discover that behaviors, thoughts and language transfer and become common. This is why who you are connected to is of utmost importance. Anyone you're attached to has a passage of influence in your life.

LIFE Expression:

otect that which is familiar because it's what we

nd we enforce popularity by ~~that which~~ we act out.

based on
~~th~~ which is popuple what

PAUSE & REFLECT. PRAY & LISTEN.

◆

What life lessons have you learned in the communities you are a member of? How have those lessons shaped your thoughts and identity?

In Communities,

We protect familiar patterns because they

are common to us. We enforce ~~popular~~ popula

before ones.

"Imagine! His left hand cradling my head, his right arm around my waist!
Oh, let me warn you, sisters in Jerusalem: Don't excite love,
don't stir it up, until the time is ripe—and you're ready."
Song of Solomon 8:3-4 (The Message Bible)

FABRICATED LOVE

The covenant of marriage is ordained by God. Within this relationship, husband and wife honor God by extending unconditional love one to another. I believe that the institution of marriage is the greatest example of God's love for man that's displayed in the earth. The responsibility of "'til death do us part" is greater than realized from the outside looking in. The true strength of the bond of love between husband and wife is tested in the many moments that happen beyond the wedding and beyond the marriage bed.

Approaching my thirties, I had what I like to call the "thirty year old itch." Many young ladies that desire to be married factor marriage and children into their life plan prior to the age of thirty. The "marry by thirty life plan," gives time for them to marry, enjoy some time with their husband and start a family before they past their preconceived child bearing age.

Pete and I worked together as Youth Ministry Leaders at church. On a romantic level, I wasn't attracted to him and I had no interest in being in a relationship with him. We spent a lot of time together working on ministry plans, and we would usually hang out casually after those sessions. Hanging out for us consisted of making late night trips to Walmart or watching TV at my place. Considering that I was still adjusting to living in a new city, navigating new relationships and new ministry responsibilities, these casual moments were welcoming and basically something to do as a pastime.

Our routine became regular, and one evening after watching a movie at my place, we spontaneously kissed. I have no idea what we were thinking or how we got to that point. Of course, this could not go any further! We were the leaders of the youth ministry, and besides, I was approaching seven years of abstinence and intended to keep it that way until marriage. Unfortunately, as time progressed and our routine didn't change, I soon found myself in a sexual relationship with Pete. I quickly learned that if your decisions don't match your intentions, your actions won't either.

> *If your decisions don't match your intentions, your actions won't either*

Pete and I continued this pattern, and I found myself at a point where I allowed my desire for sexual gratification to internally justify what I knew was wrong. My fix for this was to turn this into a relationship that would lead to marriage. At the time, my mentality was that marriage had to be the end result because my next and final sexual partner was to be my husband. Isn't it funny how we try to fix our disobedience instead of simply repenting and obeying God? Pete and I knew our actions were wrong and attempted to stop, but we thought our pull to be together was a true connection when it was actually an unhealthy sexual soul tie.

> *We try to fix our disobedience instead of simply repenting and obeying God*

Since marriage was my goal, Pete was there and I enjoyed the sex, I slapped the label of love on our unhealthy soul tie and in less than a year we were engaged to be married. He proposed in April 2004. I think in his excitement of having actually purchased the ring he was eager to propose and had not planned an elaborate proposal.

We were at my apartment and I was in the kitchen frying chicken. He came over after work so he was still in his work uniform. He entered the kitchen with the ring and asked me to marry him. Instead of saying yes, I started asking questions. *"Did you talk to Pastor?" "Have you asked my Mother?"*

I honestly can't remember if I said yes (I think I did), but I accepted the ring. I had a roommate at the time, Tiana, and she came home shortly after the proposal. She shared her news of purchasing a new car that day. I showed her the ring. We congratulated each other and resumed with a normal evening. Social media wasn't an outlet during that time so there was no status updates and no big announcements of the engagement.

In the upcoming weeks, I became engulfed and excited about planning my wedding and building my future. I discussed wedding songs and colors with my friends. In all of this excitement, I was not at all enthused about building a life with Pete.

Now that we were doing things "right," sex was off the table until we were married. Pete and I started pre-marital counseling. We really hadn't dated, and I soon learned that outside of sex we were not compatible. Honestly the longer we were involved, the sex became less enjoyable for me due to the lack of connection and compatibility.

The period of dating, getting to know each other and establishing compatibility is necessary in relationships. Two cannot walk together unless they agree. I would continually take my engagement ring off as a sign of my uneasiness with moving forward with this relationship. I wanted out, but pride and fear gripped me as I considered what everyone would think if we didn't get married. Not knowing what to do, I remained in the relationship.

About five months into our rocky engagement, I had a dream that Pete was seeing someone else. The small details of the dream were not memorable but I couldn't shake the message from the dream. Though I didn't have any evidence or had not previously had these thoughts, after the dream I felt strongly that this was true. Instead of becoming a pseudo private investigator to uncover the truth, I simply asked Pete if he was seeing someone else. He denied it. I left it alone, but didn't forget how convincing the dream was.

Pete worked close to our church, and I spent a lot of time at the ministry office. A few weeks after confronting him about seeing someone else, I saw a female leaving his job in his car. I called Pete and asked who she was and he claimed she was just a coworker that needed to use his car. I initially left it alone, but within a week there was another confrontation resulting in me having a conversation with the girl I saw in his car. The truth of the dream was confirmed. He was dating and sexually involved with this girl he worked with.

I was angry at being lied to and hurt because I took his actions as an act against me. It was strange to me at the time, but I was also concerned for the young lady he was involved with. I was concerned about how this was going to affect her. I didn't learn until later in life that although we are the recipient of actions that hurt us, we are not the cause of those actions. They have little to do with us. We act and respond from learned behaviors, good and bad. At some point, we all find ourselves on the giving and receiving end of pain.

I ended the engagement initially, but I was so stuck on making "the plan" happen that we made a brief attempt to work things out. Fortunately, reconciliation did not work. Why did I want to keep a relationship that I had no desire to be in? It was because I built such an image of what I thought my life was supposed to be in my mind that I was devastated at the thought of not having it. It wasn't an overnight fix, but my hurt and devastation were temporary. I was able to move forward accepting the responsibility and part I played in attempting to build my desired future from a relationship that never should have happened.

In moving forward, I dealt with the temptation to immediately entertain other relationships. After realizing that texts, phone calls and attention were like patches, I had to change my focus from dwelling only on my desired life. When we are consumed with our own plans we leave little to no room for God's plan.

I recommitted to practicing abstinence until marriage. In making this decision, I had to change behavioral and thought patterns. I couldn't expect different results without making changes. I began sharing my truth to help other young ladies. The freedom to share your truth is an amazing healing agent!

Seeing and experiencing healthy relationships provides us with a pattern and gives access to needed wisdom for success in relationships. I didn't grow up in a home seeing a pattern for a healthy relationship, so fulfilling my own desires was my main focus in relationships. Embracing

God's love for us provides the needed foundation to exchanging love in relationships. God's love towards us is not temporal or circumstantial. With that understanding, I have a better perspective of love in relationships. I now desire to be a conduit of God's love when I marry. My future husband has a delightful time in store for him!

LIFE Expression:
*In relationships, we duplicate what we see and
we are misguided by what we don't see.*

PAUSE & REFLECT. PRAY & LISTEN.

◆

*Consider a time that plans you made for your life did not work out.
How did that make you feel and how did you respond?*

What was your response?

_____

_____

_____

_____

_____

_____

_____

_____

_____

_____

_____

_____

_____

_____

_____

_____

_____

"For as the heavens are higher than the earth, so are My ways higher than your ways and My thoughts than your thoughts."
Isaiah 55:9

MADE TO FLY

It's amazing how you can find yourself on a path in life you would never have chosen. Sometimes, you are left with no choice but to trust God and move forward with the opportunities He presents.

In 2004, I was offered the opportunity to work full time in a paid position for the ministry offices where I volunteered for the past four years. God's Grace International (GGI) shared office space with Leading Ladies Ministry (LLM) and Toni Dowdy Ministries (TDM). I worked as Office Manager

> *Move forward with the opportunities He presents*

for the three in one operation as an employee of GGI. I loved ministry work. Days were busy with phone calls and e-mails to confirm engagements for Pastor Dowdy, making reservations for events and guests we hosted, creating and mailing flyers and letters for events, all combined with a number of other clerical and administrative tasks. Even with the daily dress code consisting of skirts and pantyhose, I looked forward to each day.

The church was thriving and growing, but it was still a young organization. After about a year, the decision was made to end the paid staff position in an effort to strengthen the financial standing of the church. I wasn't opposed to this because my desire was to see the church continue to flourish and grow.

Being faced with having to search for employment gave me a new perspective and approach. Prior to working in the ministry office, I worked in a call center starting as a Customer Service Representative and was later promoted to Reporting Analyst. Prior to the call center, I worked as a Software Trainer for a computer learning center. I really enjoyed training and was afforded several opportunities to facilitate trainings while I worked in the call center. I decided in my search for employment, I wanted to do something I enjoyed instead of just being employed for a paycheck. I loved to train and focused my job search on training positions.

I not only enjoy training, I believe it's one of my God given talents. I started my first training job in 1999 with no training experience, but was offered the position based on my training demo during the interview process. I consistently get positive feedback from my training sessions, so I'm confident when I say it's what I know I do well.

I came across a Software Consultant position that piqued my interest. It was a contract assignment and the job posting listed several cities for the training locations, including the city where I lived. I applied for the position and was contacted for an interview. To my surprise, the interview was in Virginia. They scheduled a flight for me to travel to Virginia for a face to face interview and to do a training demo. I was available and agreed to the scheduled date and time. I felt both nervous and excited as I worked on the content and materials for the training demo.

I looked forward to the possibility of having a training position again, but there was this flying part I had to deal with. Before this opportunity, I had only flown one time and that was for a trip I took to Chicago while in high school. I remember being at the airport with my mother and bursting into tears when I looked out the window of the airport and saw the massive airplane that I soon had to board. Fortunately, I made it to Chicago and back home safely, but becoming a frequent flyer was not on my agenda. My life up to this point had not demanded it, and with a recent rise in terrorist activity on airplanes I wasn't fond of it.

The day of the interview, I had an early morning flight because I was scheduled to interview and return home the same day. I arrived at the airport as an inexperienced traveler, but I made it through the processes of checking in, clearing through security and arriving at the gate with ease. As boarding time approached, I learned that the flight was delayed. There was enough time between my arrival and my interview time that I wasn't initially concerned. After being delayed for over an hour, I called the company to notify them of the flight delays. They were understanding and fine with adjusting the time of the interview if needed.

The airline staff then announced that the delay was due to mechanical issues with the airplane. Thoughts of cancelling the interview flooded my mind because I wasn't about to fly on an airplane with mechanical problems. I began to pray because I needed reassurance to stay and wait for the flight. I wanted to get out of the airport, get in my car and head home. I'm glad I chose to wait. I arrived in Virginia safely, and had a successful interview. I received a phone call offering me the position before I made it back to the airport for my return flight.

The project began with four weeks of training in Virginia. For the duration of the project I worked in Florida, Virginia and Kansas. Needless to say flying became a regular mode of transportation for me. Since then, I've continued to work as a Software Consultant and I continue to fly regularly. I have lost track of the number of flights I've taken over the years.

> *There is absolutely nothing outside of God's reach*

I'm grateful that I didn't turn around and go home that day in the airport. I had no idea what the outcome of my steps would be, but continuing forward caused me to grow and affords me countless opportunities in my career to travel. Yes, arriving to a city quickly because of flying instead of driving is convenient and I have been to cities that I didn't know existed until I was assigned to travel there. Those are definite perks, but they are not the greatest reward.

What is most rewarding for me as a frequent flyer is experiencing God from another view. Looking out of the window in an airplane intrigues and challenges me. Flying above the clouds shows me that there is absolutely nothing outside of God's reach. Seeing God's creation at another altitude reassures me of His care for me.

LIFE Expression:
Elevate your thoughts and take another look at your life.
Altitude changes the view.

PAUSE & REFLECT. PRAY & LISTEN.

◆

What new experiences have stretched your faith and changed your perspective?

_____

_____

_____

_____

_____

_____

_____

_____

_____

_____

_____

_____

_____

_____

_____

_____

_____

"Indeed God speaks once, or twice, yet no one notices it. In a dream, a vision of the night, when sound sleep falls on men, while they slumber in their beds, then He opens the ears of men, and seals their instruction."
Job 33:14-16

DISTINGUISHING DREAMS

We learn so much about God's ways and the life He has purposed for us when we read and study the Bible. God speaks to us and warns us of what is to come in various ways. Dreams are one of the many ways that He may give instructions or warn us. Science says we dream four to six times per night. I don't consider myself to be what some would call a dreamer, and I don't always write down what I dream. However, I usually take mental note of them if they are very impressionable.

I was scheduled to start a new training contract in June 2006. This was only my second contract assignment and it would include me training in dialysis facilities. Having never worked in any type of medical facility, I was both nervous and excited. The assignment included four weeks of paid training in Atlanta scheduled to start on Monday, June 5th. The week before starting, I began having a recurring dream. For three nights I dreamed that I missed my flight and could not get to the training to start the assignment. I shared the dreams with a colleague that was on the same assignment because I was so puzzled by them. I didn't feel as if I should not have accepted the assignment, but I did feel that something wasn't right. Not knowing at the time what it could be, I concluded I was just a little too anxious about this new project.

On Saturday, June 3rd, I attended our annual church picnic. We were at a location with poor cell phone reception so I left my cell phone in the car. When I left the picnic that afternoon, notifications of missed calls and voice messages from my sister and brother in Greenville started to come through on my phone. When I called my brother back I was *The course of my day quickly changed* informed that our mother (Moma) was in the hospital. Our sister, who we affectionately called Sista received a phone call from Moma earlier that morning. When she called Sista, Moma was on the floor and too weak to get up. She had been on the floor all night. Sista called my brother Sal to go to Moma's house with her. When they arrived, Sal climbed through a window since Moma couldn't get up to come to the door. They called an ambulance to take her to the hospital and she was admitted.

The course of my day quickly changed. I was two days away from the start of the new training project and without question, seeing about Moma was priority. I went to my apartment, packed an overnight bag and prepared to get on the road to head to Greenville. A friend from church took the trip with me for support. When we got there, Moma was alert and the hospital was running tests to determine what was wrong.

The next day we stayed at the hospital all day. Moma was still a little weak, but alert and talking. They still had not provided a diagnosis, but they informed us of a series of tests they were running. Since Moma was responsive and we didn't have any definite answers, I traveled back home that evening. I still needed to prepare to leave for the training that started in Atlanta the next day and my friend that traveled with me had to return to work.

Despite the recurring dream of missing my flight, I made it to Atlanta with no issues. The training was going well. I was learning new information and meeting new people. I called Sista every day to check on Moma. There was still no definite answer as to her condition, and we were still waiting on a diagnosis and plan of recovery. They were treating several small ailments in order to make a determination on what the major issue was.

I completed the first week of training and was looking forward to the weekend. The upcoming weekend was a big one for our family. We were celebrating the wedding of my nephew Seth, who is also the oldest grandchild. Since I had flown to Atlanta for the training, Sal drove from Greenville on Friday to pick me up so I could attend the wedding on Sunday. When he arrived to pick me up, he commented on how sick Moma was and that it would take some time for a full recovery. We went straight to the hospital when we arrived in Greenville.

Some of the tests revealed that Moma had kidney stones and the hospital scheduled surgery to remove them on Saturday. The visit with her on Friday was good. She still was a little weak, but talkative. I went back on Saturday to visit with her before she went in for surgery, and other family members were there also. Moma was in very good spirits. She was being comical and cracking jokes with us. After the surgery, the doctor informed us that they removed one kidney stone, but had to stop after removing about half of another one due to the amount of infection that was present. Moma didn't wake up from the anesthesia right away. We wanted her to rest, so we left the hospital for the evening with plans to visit the next day before the wedding.

A little after midnight we were called by the hospital to sign a consent form. They requested consent to insert an additional port to draw blood because they could not get any from the current port. I was staying at the home of my friend, Nina. She lived close to the hospital, so I went to the hospital to sign the consent form. Moma was on a ventilator and according to the doctor, she was not doing well. She still had not woke up from the surgery earlier that day. Out of concern from the doctor's report I called my siblings and they came to the hospital.

Moma had five children, and all of us were in town because of Seth's wedding. Sista and I were standing in the hallway while my brothers were in the room with Moma and overheard one of the hospital employees say to another,

"Have you heard about Willie?" We looked at each other, but didn't say a word. Willie is my Moma's name, and many of her caregivers knew her because she retired from the hospital she was in. After about an hour of visiting with her we left the hospital.

When I got back to Nina's house, I planned to lie down and rest. I went in the bathroom to prepare and

My only solace was to cry out to God

began to sing, "I Need You Now." As a music lover, I often hear song lyrics that fit the moment and I'll start singing. My heart was heavy from the doctor's report and my only solace was to cry out to God. I did get to lie down for a few hours before we were called to come back to the hospital around 4:00am.

By now, my thoughts were racing and though I wanted to remain hopeful, fear was setting in. When we arrived at the hospital, one of my aunts and one of my uncles was there also. The hospital staff gathered us in a room, and the doctor advised us that Moma had passed away. Tears immediately began to fall from the eyes of almost everyone in the room. We stayed in that room for a few more moments to deal with the harsh blow of the news.

We had to provide some information to the doctor about arrangements. Sista and I went to the room Moma stayed in for the week and gathered her personal belongings. Before we left the hospital, we briefly discussed Seth's wedding scheduled for that afternoon. It was decided that we would move forward with the wedding and not tell any of the grandchildren until the wedding and reception were over.

Later that morning, I drove to Walmart to pick up some personal items since I would now be staying in Greenville the remainder of the week. Thinking about Moma, I cried the entire way to the store. At one point during the drive, it felt as if my chest ripped open and my heart was torn out. Moma and I had a pivotal conversation about a week before she went into the hospital. It wasn't a deep or wisdom packed conversation. It was the first conversation that I felt we had as mother and daughter who were now friends. That role transition happens at different times based on the relationship between a mother and her daughter. Though they will always be mother, the approach and conversation is different when they accept and are at peace with their baby being a grown adult. I pulled into the parking lot at Walmart and struggled to compose myself before going in.

Preparing for the wedding that afternoon was difficult, but we knew Moma would want us to continue with it for Seth. When I arrived at the church, Seth was in the parking lot getting some things from his car. He approached the car and immediately asks, *"How's she doing?"* He wanted his "Bigma" to be at his wedding, but he also wanted her to be well. With strength I didn't realize I had, I looked at him and responded, *"She's good."*

After having to miss the entire second week of training, the recurring dreams made sense. I realized the dreams were warnings to me that something was about to happen. Though I was able to complete the last two weeks of training and continue the assignment, the start of the training collided with the most life altering event I ever experienced. As displaced as I felt in those dreams of missing the flight is how life often feels for a young woman without her mother.

Life is challenging. Growing as a young woman is challenging. However, challenging isn't a strong enough word to express the feeling of experiencing life as a young woman without your mother. After that loss, life is never the same. No amount of love and support from others compares to the love and presence of your mother. I realize everyone may not have had their mother's love and support but for those that have, it is truly a rare love.

LIFE Expression:
Time and moments are fleeting.
Be attentive and love with abandon.

PAUSE & REFLECT. PRAY & LISTEN.

◆

In what ways does God warn you about things to come in your life?

_____

_____

_____

_____

_____

_____

_____

_____

_____

_____

_____

_____

_____

_____

_____

> *"For our struggle is not against flesh and blood, but against the rulers, against the powers, against the world forces of this darkness, against the spiritual forces of wickedness in the heavenly places."*
> Ephesians 6:12

FUTILELY FIGHTING

Growing up with three older brothers, I often playfully wrestled with the youngest of the three. As a girl, when you wrestle with an older brother, you believe you can contend with almost anyone. On a few occasions I carried this behavior outside of the home resulting in a few fist fights at school and on the school bus. In the neighborhood I grew up in, a fight was the final response to any escalated conflict. The easy thing about fighting when you're a child is that the fight resolved the conflict and relationships resumed quickly.

> *It's tempting to take matters into our own hands*

As long as we engage in relationships on any level with others, we will experience moments of conflict in those relationships. As adults and Christians we have to learn effective conflict resolution because childhood fights are no longer an option. Prayer is our greatest weapon in conflict. Prayer shouldn't become so routine that we neglect to make it priority. We don't always see an immediate change when we pray, so it's tempting to take matters into our own hands.

Being a part of an organization from its inception has the tendency to give you a deeper affection towards it. I have been in church all my life, so attending church is familiar for me. The experience at God's Grace International (GGI) was different because I was part of the formation meeting and one of the original members. As the church progressed, I served as Church Administrator and on the Board of Directors. From seeing large crowds skim down, benevolence taken advantage of and enduring a church split, I learned to weather the storms and stand with the vision and visionary that I believed I was called to stand with. I reached a point where my mindset became "this too shall pass" because we withstood every other test.

A storm came in the last quarter of 2009 that was different than any other. Knowing that leaders are touched by the storm before it reaches those attached to them, I can't imagine the sting of the blows Pastor Dowdy experienced since starting GGI. If you're a person that's constantly helping and giving, it may feel like reciprocation and recompense are scarce. When you eagerly desire change, desperation can cause you to accept counterfeits even with red flags popping up like a minefield. It is true that there are situations that arise where you can't predict how you will respond.

Because of Pastor Dowdy's tenure and travel in ministry over the years, she had numerous long standing relationships with ministry leaders in various locations. She often extended herself to aid in the development and growth of other ministries while trusting God with the needs of her own. Many leaders, pastors and ministers looked to her for counsel and guidance. GGI had an established community of churches that we regularly supported and fellowshipped with. These churches and their pastors also provided great support to GGI. The pastors and their parishioners had become our extended family.

In 2009, Bishop Wilcox *(pronounced wil-cŏh)* was introduced to Pastor Dowdy through mutual acquaintances. His claim was that he was sent to help and be a son to her. He wanted to help care for her personally and help grow her ministries and the church. Her only biological child had recently passed away, and she fully received him in this role in her life. He immediately began to shower her with gifts and frequent services that were hosted by GGI and the other churches in our community. We also began to support his events. He had an established organization of churches that he served as bishop as well as a church that he served as pastor. They were small churches and some were newly formed.

It was interesting that as people learned of Pastor Dowdy's relationship with Bishop Wilcox, we started hearing reports of previous encounters that other leaders had with him. They were mostly negative reports. Leaders that have known Pastor Dowdy for years called with warnings and concern about her relationship with him. They advised her to cut ties immediately and some even said he was suspected to be a con artist. Pastor Dowdy wanted to give him an opportunity to prove who he was instead of making a decision based on the words of others, so she continued in relationship with him.

Bishop Wilcox was a lively person. Services with him were laced with loud music, extravagant prophecies and numerous offerings. The more we attended services with him, the more evident it became that the warnings Pastor Dowdy received about him should not be ignored. His actions were often questionable and mysterious. However, it wasn't acceptable to openly question his actions no matter how strange they were. I'll share a little of what we experienced from him to explain why his behavior was questionable. A full list would be too exhaustive.

Bishop Wilcox was married to a much younger woman. In several services his wife would excuse herself for periods of time, often crying for no apparent reason and her countenance was usually sad. Shortly after we met him, he hosted the annual convocation for his organization. Within six months of that event, every church and leader under his organization broke ties with him and the organization. He suddenly decided to leave the church he served as pastor to start a new church in another city. This included him leaving his wife to start dating and eventually living with a young lady in his new church while he was still married. He was the Founder, President and Instructor of a seminary school where he awarded Bachelors, Masters and Doctorate degrees in as little as six months. At one of the graduation ceremonies we attended, he randomly selected a student as Valedictorian to have them come up and speak.

The more his true character was revealed through his actions, the more warnings Pastor Dowdy received. Unfortunately, no matter how questionable his actions were, his influence was strong. He convinced Pastor Dowdy that anyone that spoke against him in any way was his enemy, and because of her alliance with him she shouldn't have relationship with his enemies. After a few months of his influence, Pastor Dowdy cut ties with the churches and leaders that GGI regularly fellowshipped with.

Pastor Dowdy and I talked almost daily. We talked about church and ministry business or just to check on one another. She would share her concerns about his behavior with me, and I voiced my concerns to her. She would in turn share these discussions with Bishop Wilcox so he knew what others were saying about him. I believe she shared with him in order to relieve the doubts and questions she had about his behavior. Pastor Dowdy had a great deal of hope in the outcome of her relationship with Bishop Wilcox and desired to see all the promises he made come to fruition.

My futile efforts were not working Her hope drew her closer to him and began to drive a wedge in her relationships with others, including her relationship with me. Because of my love for her and

39

GGI I wanted to protect her and the church from any greater loss than we already experienced. I was fighting for the truth to prevail, but not fighting correctly. My fighting included talking to Pastor Dowdy about my concerns more than I prayed about them. My fighting included me researching information on Bishop Wilcox to prove the falsehood in the exhaustive biography he presented including several degrees from institutions he had not attended and churches he established that had no proof of existing. My futile efforts were not working.

Bishop Wilcox now wanted Pastor Dowdy to bring GGI under his organization. Since all the churches that were originally under his organization left, there technically was no organization, it was just him. Being a part of his organization required annual dues from EVERY member in our church. The amount depended on your title or position so there was a push to issue ministerial credentials to several of us in the church.

Pastor Dowdy scheduled a church meeting to discuss GGI becoming a part of his organization. Prior to the meeting, board members were given information packets about his organization for review. We were given the directive from Pastor Dowdy to address all of our concerns and to ask questions in the meeting with him. We were told that she only wanted to move forward with it if it was beneficial for the church. The packet was full of red flags. It wasn't an authentic document. It was copied from another organization, and noticeably so because the name wasn't updated on some of the pages. The benefits and offerings listed in this document as being provided by his organization were like apples hanging from a grapevine. They were not real.

The evening of the meeting, I based my questions on the obvious misrepresentation in the information packet. My hope was still that the truth would surface and prevail so we could successfully move beyond this situation. The more questions I asked, the more Bishop Wilcox became combative. He attempted to twist my words to the point where we had to play back the recording of the meeting to prove what was said. Again my fighting was futile. When Pastor Dowdy spoke up, it was in defense of Bishop Wilcox. In that moment, I felt like a sheep in the presence of a hungry wolf with the shepherd present, but pushing me towards the wolf instead of covering me.

Though that was a blow, I had to regain my footing. I am worth fighting for. You are worth fighting for. Never forget to protect yourself before fighting for someone else. It was evident that their decision had been made before this meeting. We had not been called together to discuss this potential change, we were being informed of the inevitable change.

LIFE Expression
When what or who you're fighting for does not fight for you,
it's time to reevaluate.

PAUSE & REFLECT. PRAY & LISTEN.
◆

When have you used the wrong approach or strategy in a battle?
What was the outcome?

_____

_____

_____

_____

_____

_____

_____

_____

_____

_____

_____

_____

_____

_____

_____

_____

_____

"⁴You shall not make for yourself an idol, or any likeness of what is in heaven above or on the earth beneath or in the water under the earth. ⁵You shall not worship them or serve them; for I, the Lord your God, am a jealous God..."
Exodus 20:4, 5

REESTABLISHED ORDER

Powerful storms leave significant damage and unearth what's hidden. When the foundation is shaken, damage results that exposes flaws in the building process. This is true in building structures and relationships.

It had only been about four months of Bishop Wilcox being around, but the impact and damage felt like years. The impact on my relationship with Pastor Dowdy was most difficult for me to adjust to. She was not only a pastor to me, she was a mother figure. Three and a half years had passed since Moma's death, and that made my relationship with Pastor Dowdy even more meaningful. It had been over ten years since I connected with Pastor Dowdy and her influence shaped many of my ideals as a young woman.

What I exalted was crumbling During those years, I fully embraced the community, I spoke the language and I wore the acceptable attire. I only missed services or events if I was out of town for work. As an inaugural member of God's Grace International (GGI) I was sure that these were my people, this was my church and I was fighting for us. I was not sure about who was fighting for me, who I had become and who I was really serving.

After almost ten years of prioritizing church, ministry and my pastor above everything, having to acknowledge that my priorities were out of order and required adjusting was a painful truth to face. It got to the point where I battled depression and had to see my doctor for stress related chest pains. Internally my body was responding to the truth that I had yet to acknowledge and embrace. I shared with Pastor Dowdy what was going on with my health, and she made light of it. She said I was just feeling left out and I would be alright. Wow, another blow!

I was nearing a breaking point. It usually takes a lot for me to cry. Not the sentimental tear drops over a movie, television show or love story. I can drop those fairly easy. I'm talking about really crying and releasing the emotions of the moment. I don't do that often, but when I do it's an event. It's a big, long event and there's nothing cute about it.

Excerpt from my journal dated December 29, 2009

GOD!!! ...I ask Your forgiveness and I repent because I feel I allowed my focus to get off of You and establishing/ strengthening my relationship with You. Instead I focused on service in ministry and my relationship with my pastor. I'm so sorry Lord. ...So now I find myself in what feels like a very dark place. I feel more alone than I have ever felt...

I realized the focus of my affection was misguided and what I exalted was crumbling. *How did I even get to this place?* I religiously served and gave, yet God was displaced in my world. I faced that reality. I acknowledged it. I accepted it. I cried.

I usually want and need to be alone when I cry, but this time was different. I composed myself enough to get up and go to the bathroom. I looked at myself in the mirror and saw the pain in my bloodshot red eyes. My internal cry for help prevailed. I took a picture of how I looked at that moment and texted Tiana. Though we were no longer roommates, we were still close friends. She called me immediately and although I couldn't fully express what was wrong, I didn't have to. She came to my apartment and stayed for hours. We talked, she made me laugh as always, and she didn't leave until she felt I was alright.

That moment was pivotal for me. That moment showed me that I needed to start making decisions to redirect my affection. Tiana had plans to travel to Florida to bring in the New Year and spend time with family, and she invited me to go. Church service at God's Grace International (GGI) was always priority for me, so missing an event like New Year's Eve service was unheard of, until now. I accepted the invitation to go on the trip to Florida.

On New Year's Eve, Tiana and I were out running errands and preparing to get on the road. At one of the stops we made I waited in the car, and there was a store across the street from where we were. I glanced across the street and saw Pastor Dowdy and a young lady from GGI pull up and go into the store. They were also about to get on the road. They were traveling to attend service with Bishop Wilcox. Seeing this caused a flood of emotions.

For so many years I'd been right beside Pastor Dowdy and I temporarily felt out of place. My heart sank and began to hurt. I didn't want to be sad during this trip and cause others to not enjoy themselves, so I needed help coping with what I was feeling. I had a prayer book with me, and most of the trip to Florida I sat quietly and read prayers while asking God to heal my heart. Tiana drove and periodically asked me how I was doing and if I was OK. She didn't know what I saw before we left and I never told her. She knew that making this trip was big for me and she hoped that this getaway would help.

We stayed in Florida for three days and it was so refreshing. The time away was a prescribed balm for me. The services were encouraging, the food was delicious and the laughter was needed. The trip was full and overflowing with genuine love from

> *I could no longer engage in this fight*

Tiana's family and great wisdom from her cousin that pastors a flourishing church in Florida. He is an ordained bishop with several churches under his organization. I spoke with him briefly about what I was experiencing at GGI. I still hoped for change in the situation with Bishop Wilcox. I was grasping for any lifeline that could help because the fighter in me didn't want to accept that I could no longer engage in this fight.

The trip to Florida was a precursor to the healing process and strength for the months ahead. I continued to choose moments to get away including some weekends to enjoy time with family and friends. I had not done that in the past, so I began to allow myself to shift my priorities.

At GGI, church services continued to be awkward when Bishop Wilcox was present. I use the term "twilight zone" to describe those times. It reached the point that we never knew what he was going to do or say or how Pastor Dowdy would act or react in his presence. I would have never believed that things would have gotten to this point if I wasn't experiencing it. Even with the drastic changes, I remained at GGI. I still believed that God connected me to Pastor Dowdy and He had not instructed me to leave.

My relationship with Pastor Dowdy continued to be strained. She called me one day and shared with me that other volunteer office staff told her I compromised confidential church files. This was completely false because I password protected confidential files and did not share the files or passwords. During this conversation she mentioned the possibility of me being sat down from my position in the office or me leaving the church.

While hearing all of this, I was emotionally backed in a corner in that a moment. I felt as if she was urging me to leave the church. I was insulted that we were discussing these lies as if she didn't know me and know my character. I was frustrated and wanted to respond in my emotions, but I audibly heard the words, *She's going to need you.* God speaks to me like that sometimes. It's so audible and such an interjection in the moment that I know it's Him. Those words calmed me. Those words were the only instructions I had in this situation. Those words caused me to remain in place to ride out this storm.

LIFE Expression:
Allowing God to be properly positioned in our lives keeps us open to hearing Him above the noise of distractions.

PAUSE & REFLECT. PRAY & LISTEN.

Think of a time when you realized your life and priorities were out of order. How was it corrected?

_____

_____

_____

_____

_____

_____

_____

_____

_____

_____

_____

_____

_____

_____

_____

"Have I not commanded you? Be strong and courageous. Do not be afraid; do not be discouraged, for the LORD your God will be with you wherever you go."
Joshua 1:9

<hr>

NECESSARY TRANSITION

All that God does and allows is with purpose. A situation can look muddled or cloudy to us, but it's crystal clear to Him because He knows the end from the beginning.

One night in March 2010, I was awakened over in the morning by excruciating abdominal pain. The best way I can describe the pain is imagine being kicked in the stomach by a football player. Yes, it was that severe. It didn't occur every night, but over the next thirty to forty-five days I had a few more episodes like that. From trying medicine I had at home to making a trip to Walmart at 3:00am to search for other medication, I sought any type of relief from this unimaginable pain. The medicine did not help. The only thing that helped was curling up in a fetal position in bed and waiting or hoping to fall back to sleep until the pain subsided.

On Tuesday, May 4, 2010, I was at work and had just returned from lunch break when I felt the pain coming on. This was the first time it happened during the day, but I knew with the severity of the pain I had to leave work. I notified my manager and left the office. When I left work, I called my doctor's office. My doctor wasn't available, but there was another doctor available so I went straight there. The doctor didn't run any tests, but diagnosed the pain as acid reflux. He gave me samples of medication to treat acid reflux and sent me home. I took the medicine immediately and waited a few hours, but had no relief.

On my way home from the doctor, I called Tiana and she came to my apartment to check on me. After seeing that the medicine wasn't helping, she suggested I go to the emergency room. I agreed and she took me to the hospital. The medical staff ran tests and discovered I had numerous stones in my gallbladder, and the painful episodes were gallbladder attacks.

The suggested remedy by the doctor was surgery to remove the entire organ. I asked if there was any alternative to surgery or completely removing my gallbladder. The doctor advised that if my gallbladder wasn't removed, I would continue to develop stones and have gallbladder attacks. By now it was early Wednesday morning. The first available time for surgery was Thursday morning so they admitted me and I spent Wednesday night in the hospital.

I had never had surgery before, nor stayed overnight in a hospital. I was scared and wished more than anything that Moma was still living to be there with me. Fortunately, Sista drove from Greenville and stayed with me at the hospital Wednesday night. She didn't leave until I was released from the hospital after surgery on Thursday. Tiana stayed until she had to leave to go to work Wednesday morning and she came back Thursday before I went back for surgery. Pastor Dowdy came to visit on Wednesday. While there, she received a call from Bishop Wilcox. She started telling him about me being in the hospital and I shook my head to indicate I didn't want this shared with him. I didn't feel he was truly interested in my well being so there was no reason to inform him. She told him anyway. Pastor Dowdy came back on Thursday morning and prayed for me before surgery. She waited with Sista until I was out of surgery.

The surgery was outpatient and I was released later that day. My apartment had stairs so Minister Loman offered for me to come stay at her house until I was well enough to walk up and down stairs. She allowed me to sleep in her bedroom while she slept in the den because someone else was living with her and occupying her guest bedroom. That Sunday was Mother's Day, and I had a few visits from friends and family, including my brother Sal and his wife. Minister Loman was gone until late evening because she spent the day with Pastor Dowdy and Bishop Wilcox. When she returned home that evening, she entered the bedroom where I was. I was preparing to retire for the evening and already lying in the bed.

She came and stood beside the bed and said, *"When are you going home? I'm ready to have my bed back."* Though alarmed by her question and statement since I had only been there a few days, I simply responded, *"I'll go home tomorrow."*

53

In the exchange with Minister Loman, home was back to my apartment. However, when she left the room I heard very clearly, *You need to move back home*. I knew that home in this context was back to Greenville. There was no one else in the room, but this was a clear and audible interruption of my current thought so it definitely caught my attention. Yes, the past few months had been trying, but moving was not on my mind or agenda. I was certain I was where I was supposed to be and sure this is where God placed me. I began to pray because I felt as if this could not be God.

The next morning Pastor Dowdy came to Minister Loman's for a visit. Her conversation with me like many of our recent ones, quickly turned to Bishop Wilcox and his role in her life and God's Grace International (GGI). There was a gradual deterioration in GGI since Bishop Wilcox's arrival. Some church members began to skip service if they knew he would be there. *"He'll be coming to speak every fourth Sunday. Those that don't want to be there when he speaks, don't have to come,"* she said. This was her stance and I didn't rebuttal.

When Pastor Dowdy left, I was reminded of the words I heard the night before, *You need to move back home*. I was overwhelmed and moved to tears. I went into the bedroom and called a close friend of mine, Lori. I shared with her my dilemma about moving home. After hearing my heart, she encouraged me to obey God over my feelings. We ended the call and I texted a few family members to get their thoughts on my moving home. Everyone responded with excitement including Sista. Sista offered to ask her husband, Paul, if I could stay with them until I found a place of my own if I decided to move back. With much to ponder, I left Minister Loman's home that day and went back to my apartment.

> **I thought this storm would pass**

Though a move was not in my plans, it looked as if things were falling in place. The timing was good. It was May, and my lease was ending in June. My current roommate, Bev, was already planning to move to her own place when the lease ended. However, there was still my job and the church. Though things had not been going well at GGI, it was not my intention to completely disconnect. I thought this storm would pass like many others in the past, so moving would allow me to distance myself. It was the perfect solution. I could move back to Greenville and still attend church service on Sunday. There were several members that commuted to GGI; some traveled three hours one way so an hour and half for me was doable.

My post-surgery visit to the doctor went well and I was already feeling better. I wasn't yet cleared to drive, but I was recovering well and could get out of the house some. Saturday, I attended a concert with a friend. After the concert, they were heading out of town and happened to be going to a city near where my friend April lived. April also attended GGI. I arranged to ride out of town with them and for April to pick me up. The plan was to stay over with April and ride to church with her on Sunday. All went as planned on Saturday but Sunday held a sudden turn of events.

The ride to church from April's house was about an hour and half so I woke up early on Sunday to prepare since I was still moving a little slow from surgery. When I returned to the bedroom from the bathroom, I looked at my phone and realized that I missed a call from Pastor Dowdy. *I had not seen or spoken with her since her visit at minister Loman's.*

She left a voice message, but before I could listen to it, I received a text message from her that read, "*I am no longer your pastor. Send your keys by Bev.*" She was referring to the keys I held to the church. Sarah, who also worked in the church office, borrowed my keys earlier in the week so I didn't have them. I responded to the text to inform her that Sarah had the keys and she could get them from her.

When I listened to the voice message, the words she texted were repeated along with false accusations of me having already cleaned out my things in the office. I called her back but the truth wasn't being heard. Anything items that I had in the office or stored anywhere in the church was still there and I never went back to retrieve it. them I was too emotionally exhausted by all that transpired over the past several months to immediately say anything else.

April was still lying down because she wasn't feeling well. I decided to lay back down and didn't even say anything to April right away about the text. After about thirty minutes I got back up and went to the other room to tell April what happened. She was completely shocked. She said, *"What!? How did you get put out and church hasn't even started yet?"* We both laughed at her response, but really had no understanding of what was going on.

At that point all we knew was that we didn't have to make the trip to church that morning. Since neither of us was at service, we learned later that Pastor Dowdy met with the congregation after church and informed them of my release. They were advised that anyone else not on board with Bishop Wilcox was free to leave.

The release from GGI not only became my release to move, but the release to move with complete freedom from the situation. I spoke with my manager about working remotely. He said the option was available if I decided to move. There were so many emotions that accompanied this pending transition. Because of the way I was put out of the church I served in from its inception, I was hurt and angry. A text and voice message is NOT the most effective way for adults to communicate about their relationships. I was suddenly disconnected from the organization and people I had been a part of for over ten years. I had no vision for my life beyond serving Pastor Dowdy in ministry and I was uncertain about the days ahead.

The depth of my hurt was exposed in a church service. Tiana wasn't a member at GGI and I went to an evening service at the church she attended. There was a guest preacher that evening. During the altar call, the preacher asked for anyone experiencing church hurt to come to the altar. I heard the call and having heard the term, "church hurt" before I was certain this wasn't me. However, my legs thought different. In the next moment I'm walking down that long aisle to get to the altar while saying to myself, *Why are you going up here? You came straight from work and you look bad! You have on pants and you're going to the front of this church! WHAT are you doing?*

> **The depth of my hurt was exposed**

My mental arguments didn't win. I arrived at the altar and was met with prayers and embraces. When I left service that evening, I started to accept my new reality as truth. I accepted that yes, I was put out of a church and I am hurting. I knew I could not move forward feeling this way. Through the pain, anger and disappointment, I had to forgive Pastor Dowdy.

The day that I left the office I worked in for the last time, the song "No Looking Back" was playing on the radio. When I pulled out of the parking garage, I decided to call Pastor Dowdy to express how I felt and to say, "I forgive you." During the phone call I was able to get those words out, but unfortunately the focus of the conversation again turned to Bishop Wilcox.

The call was brief with no resolution and no sincere apologies. The once close knit relationship we had could now only be measured by the tension felt during that brief exchange. The conversation ended with her saying, *"I'm happier than I've ever been. I have my son (Bishop Wilcox) and soon to have a new daughter (the young lady he was dating)."* That was her exit out of my life and would be the last time I spoke with her for a few years.

After planting my life where I thought I was destined to be, I was heading back home. I was just as uncertain about what was ahead as I was when I moved ten years prior. Because of the words I heard pointing me back in that direction, I had to believe and be confident that God was with me.

LIFE Expression:
Change is inevitable. Welcome the transition that follows change so your direction will always be forward.

PAUSE & REFLECT. PRAY & LISTEN.
◆

Consider a time when you had to deal with unsolicited change. How did you handle it and what was your response?

_____

_____

_____

_____

_____

_____

_____

_____

_____

_____

_____

_____

_____

_____

_____

_____

_____

_____

"¹⁸Remember not the former things, nor consider the things of old. ¹⁹Behold, I am doing a new thing; now it springs forth, do you not perceive it? I will make a way in the wilderness and rivers in the desert."
Isaiah 43:18, 19

EMBRACING THE NEW

God has prepared places and relationships for us beyond our current circle and environment. When we have settled into conditions, it's sometimes hard to trust Him beyond that place of comfort. Whether you are facing planned or unplanned transition, trust what God allows.

June 2010, I moved back to Greenville and moved in temporarily with Sista and her family. This was not at all my plan, but God knew what was ahead. It was a huge adjustment living with Sista, her husband Paul, and their sons Timothy and Tyler. Moving from my own place to now just having my own room was different. I didn't complain because the move was so sudden and I was grateful for the open door.

Though I wasn't interested in joining a church right away, I attended church regularly with Sista and her family. My oldest brother, Sal, and his wife Phera, along with their son Seth and his family attended the same church. Most Sundays we would all go out to eat together after church. I enjoyed these moments with family that I had not had in a long time.

I like to cook, so some Sundays I would prepare dinner for the family. Everyone would come to Sista's for dinner and we ate and laughed while making wonderful memories as a family. I usually cook big meals, and I start cooking the night before. Sista would join me in the kitchen to lend a hand with prepping the food. Cooking, shopping, attending various events and numerous conversations were shared with Sista while I was living with them.

With her being almost eight years older than me, we had not shared a lot of fun moments growing up. Being the big sister, she often had to braid my hair, cook and look after me. Times of us just hanging out as sisters were rare. After our mother passed away in 2006, I would stay with Sista and her family when I came home for holidays. With me now being in the house with them, we developed a relationship as adult sisters. I was grateful for this beautiful relationship with her. Next to mothers, I believe sisters are the most important women in our lives.

While adjusting to my new life in Greenville, I realized how much of my life and time was previously consumed by church and ministry activities. Because of my love for music, I took advantage of this additional time to attend more live music events. In July 2010, one of my favorite artists, Bryon, was coming to Greenville. I thought, *Wow! What a way to welcome me back home God.*

This would be my second time seeing him perform live. In August 2009, April and I traveled to Florida to see him perform for her birthday. We were able to meet him and spend a little time with him after the show. Believe it or not, I had a complete fan meltdown when we first met him! It was an unforgettable experience that can't really be explained. When I told April he was coming to Greenville, she and her mother decided to come up for the event. Some of my friends in Greenville attended also. It was definitely great seeing him perform again. I sang loudly to the songs I knew and was pleasantly surprised with new music he shared.

It goes without saying, I'm an extreme fan of Bryon's music. Having more time now, I was able to travel to other cities to see him again later in the year. As time passed, I began to develop a rapport with his manager, Kai. After one of the shows, I was able to spend a little time with them, and I had another fan moment. He and Kai rode with me back to Greenville because they were meeting family there. Of course I could not wait to call April and say, *"Guess who was in my car!"* I continued to attend Bryon's shows when I could. Seeing him perform never gets old.

In January 2011, Bryon was performing at a few events in Charlotte. Kai personally invited me

I had to fight the mental stereotypes

to join them for the weekend and I graciously accepted. It was encouraging to be welcomed as family with his ministry team. Most of the relationships I had with people that attended God's Grace International (GGI) ended by default once I was released from there. My heart was full of gratitude for the new relationships with Kai, Bryon and the rest of the team. Even with the excitement of new relationships, I had to closely embrace people that didn't dress and think like me. I had to fight the mental stereotypes I developed over the years of how church people ~~Christians~~ should look and act. We don't realize what we're lacking until we're exposed to it.

April 2011, I was invited to travel and go on tour with Bryon and team for a span of about ten days. As needed, I would help Kai with administrative tasks such as following up on booking requests. I would also help with CD inventory and sales. The tour dates happened to include my birthday, so again I'm thinking, *Wow, God! Happy Birthday to me!* Having become family in a short span of time with an artist I admired for years was nothing I could have made happen on my own if I tried. I had no idea what life would be like for me beyond the move. Though I was still healing and adjusting in areas, I was in awe of what God was doing in my life in these new moments.

I informed Sista of the tour dates so she would know how long I would be gone. I had to drive to Atlanta to meet with the rest of the team to travel to our first destination. When I arrived, I called Sista to let her know I arrived safely to Atlanta. We were delayed with leaving, and I don't know why but I began to feel uneasy. I considered backing out of going, getting in my car and driving back to Greenville. I discounted the feeling as me being nervous about traveling this distance and this length of time with people I didn't know well. Some of the team for the tour I was meeting for the first time. I was also nervous about leaving my car parked on the street in a neighborhood I had not been in before. Though still feeling uneasy, I decided to go on the tour.

The tour was an amazing and unforgettable experience! We were in various cities in Ohio and spent one night in Chicago. The event in Chicago was streamed live so I made sure to tell Sista to watch. The night before we were heading back home, I received a phone call from Pastor Carlson. I met Pastor Carlson years ago through Leading Ladies Ministry (LLM), but had not spoken with her in several months. She said that I was on her heart and she was just checking on me. I let her know that I was out of town with friends, and I remember saying to her, *"As far as I know, everything is alright."* Though I had tucked it away, this phone call reminded me of the feeling I had earlier that something was going to happen.

During our travel back to Atlanta we experienced minor vehicle damage at a gas station and a few hours later, we had a blow out on the highway. Both situations could have been worse but thankfully no one was hurt and we arrived safely in Atlanta the morning of Tuesday, April 12th. Having felt that something was going to happen, I was eager to lay eyes on my car. To my relief, I found it exactly the way I left it. I then assumed that the incidents we had on the way home were what had me feeling uneasy. I got in my car and drove safely back to Greenville from Atlanta. I smiled and sang the entire trip home.

Allowing God to display the prepared road He has for us is difficult especially if we keep trying to chart courses without consulting Him. God has designed a unique path for your life. Trust your tour guide and enjoy the scenery. He orchestrates the most memorable moments.

> *He orchestrates the most memorable moments*

LIFE Expression:
There is both risk and reward in
letting people in and in letting people go.

PAUSE & REFLECT. PRAY & LISTEN.

◆

Consider a time when you had to adapt to new surroundings and people. How well did you adapt? What challenges did you have with adapting?

_____

_____

_____

_____

_____

_____

_____

_____

_____

_____

_____

_____

_____

_____

_____

_____

It's the way it jerks your neck
~~this~~ the way body

"3When I look at your heavens, the work of your fingers, the moon and the stars, which you have set in place, 4what is man that you are mindful of him, and the son of man that you care for him?"
Psalm 8:3, 4

◆ ◆ ◆

UNMERITED MINDFULNESS

It may not be daily that thoughts of you grace the mind of others. That is not the case with God. He is mindful of you. God is completely aware and attentive to every detail of your life. Because He knows the end from the beginning, He orders our steps with the end in mind.

There was nothing too different about that Tuesday when I returned home from being on tour with Bryon. I worked from home and had a small desk setup in the bedroom I occupied at Sista's house. Since I wasn't home for my birthday, Sista left a birthday card for me on my desk.

> *He orders our steps with the end in mind*

When she got home from work that day, she came to the door of my room smiling and said, *"Well, well, well!"* That was her way of letting me know she was glad to see me. I thanked her for the card, and we chatted a little about my trip. Later that evening, Sista's youngest son, Tyler, decided to come in my room and hangout until it was time for him to go to bed. I guess he missed me too.

69

Wednesday April 13th started as another regular day. Sista came home on her lunch break and I was in my room preparing for a conference call. I stepped out of my room and brought my laptop out to show her some of the pictures from the tour. We initially were standing in the hallway and I had to run back to my desk for a moment so I told her she could take the laptop. She took it in their bedroom and continued to scroll through the pictures while she ate lunch.

When I could break away, I joined her to talk about some of the pictures. She got to one of them of me and one of the musicians and asked, *"Who is that?"* I told her who he was and we continued to look through the pictures.

I noticed a black graduation gown hanging in their room and I asked her who it belonged to. She replied, *"That's Timothy's."* Timothy is her oldest son and he was graduating from high school that year. She was more quiet than usual, but I didn't think much of it. I had to go back to my room and get on the conference call. A few minutes later, I saw her walking down the steps leaving to head back to work.

A couple of hours passed and the boys were home from school, both in their rooms. I have a habit of keeping the ringer off on my cell phone so I didn't realize Sista's husband, Paul, had called me. When I didn't answer my phone, he called Timothy's phone and asked to speak to me. He told me that Sista had been rushed to the hospital and I needed to come. I quickly got myself and the boys in the car and we headed to the hospital.

While en route to the hospital I called my sister in law, Phera, and she and my brother Sal headed to the hospital also. I prayed as I drove to the hospital because I had no idea what could have happened for Sista to be rushed to the hospital. She worked at the highway department and since it's a public place, I wondered if there was an incident that caused her harm. When we arrived at the hospital, Paul and his cousin were standing outside. Paul was crying. When Timothy saw Paul crying, he burst into tears which then made Tyler start crying. At this point, I still don't know what is going on.

Sal and Phera arrived while we were still in the car. When they get out the car Sal sees Paul crying, and he starts crying. I'm still in the car trying to console Timothy and their cousin comes over and helps so that we can get out the car. We still don't know what happened and we don't know Sista's condition. There was a helicopter there and Paul thought that she was in there and because no one had come out, he thought she had passed.

A few minutes later, another helicopter lands. Sista was in that one. They bring her out and as they are rushing her inside, we run towards them to get some answers. Paul asked if she was alive and they told him that she was. He looks to us and informs us that she's still alive. Temporarily relieved, we all run inside to wait to hear from the doctor. I stepped away from the waiting area and called other family members to let them know what was going on.

The initial report from the doctor said it looked as if she had a stroke because of the blood on her brain but they were still running tests. Additional family members, church members and some of Sista's coworkers arrived at the hospital as we were waiting for more information. I also called some of my friends to inform them and ask them to pray. Tiana was one of the friends I called. While on the phone with her, she asked if I was ok.

Up to that point I had been strong and remained prayerful, but after her question I immediately burst into tears and said, *"I don't want my sister to die!"* She responded *"Let me get D (her son) situated and I'm on my way."* This sudden turn of events explained the feeling I had about something happening and the unexpected phone call from Pastor Carlson.

I went back to the waiting area and a few minutes later, the doctor came back out and explained that an aneurysm had ruptured on Sista's brain and that there was nothing they could do. We didn't want to accept that news and we continued to pray. He returned a few moments later and said he could do surgery. The surgery was scheduled for the next day, so me and Paul stayed overnight at the hospital. Tiana drove up to Greenville and stayed overnight at the hospital with me. Paul's mother came to town to stay at the house with Timothy and Tyler.

Sista made it through surgery, but other health issues caused additional complications during recovery. She wasn't recovering or progressing as we desired and the prognosis wasn't favorable. Over the next several days, I lived at the hospital. During this time family and extended family continued to fast, pray and cry out to God for a miracle.

It was now Tuesday, April 19th, and Paul had to make a decision whether to keep her on life support or not. After meeting with me and my brothers he let us know what he was going to do based on what he knew Sista would want. I had gone downstairs to the chapel after the meeting and then I went and sat on a bench outside the hospital.

Moments later my brother Ron came outside. They had taken Sista off of life support. I looked at him and he shook his head letting me know she didn't make it. I felt completely deflated. It was as if the wind had literally been knocked out of me. I recall my friend Nina being there, but I honestly don't remember when she arrived. She went back into the hospital and gathered my belongings out of the waiting area that had been my living space the past six days.

My niece, Sara was there also. She drove me from the hospital to Sal's house. When we arrived at Sal's, I sat

I felt completely deflated

outside on the steps. I could not stop crying. I knew that even though this was not the outcome we were praying for, that God is still sovereign and I resolved to continue to trust Him. Only He knew when I moved home in June 2010 that Sista would pass away a brief ten months later.

I remember the emotional highs and lows I experienced after she passed. I felt complete joy at times knowing that she had obtained the prize of eternal life in God's presence that we as Christians hope for. Then I would feel the pain of the reality of irrevocable change in my life and family with her being gone. After years of her being gone, it's still hard to believe at times. I have moments when I think, *Did that really happen?*

Though I left an ugly situation and it was not my initial desire to move or disconnect from God's Grace International (GGI) or Pastor Dowdy, I'm so grateful that things happened the way they did. Moving back home caused my attention to be completely where it needed to be for what was ahead. God is so mindful of me! Even when I didn't do everything right, He caused things to work out for my good.

The last ten months of life with Sista, we had a beautiful relationship. We talked, shared, and spent a lot of time together. Our relationship was more beautiful than ever before. It was as if God reconciled the ten years I was away in those ten months I lived with her before she passed.

There's a peace that comes and rests when you know and experience God's love in a dark place.

LIFE Expression:
*God's sovereignty isn't weakened in
moments beyond our control.*

PAUSE & REFLECT. PRAY & LISTEN.
◆

Recall a time when God's love for you was a ray of light in a dark situation. What was the situation? How did seeing God in it change your perspective?

_____

_____

_____

_____

_____

_____

_____

_____

_____

_____

_____

_____

_____

_____

_____

_____

"But there is nothing covered up that will not be revealed,
and hidden that will not be known."
Luke 12:2

────────────◆──────◆──────◆────────────

TRUTH REVEALED

Hello God, I'm still here! That was my thought as I realized I was now doing life without Moma, Pastor Dowdy and Sista. These three had been the dominant female voices in my life, and I was feeling stripped and lost. I was certain I had dropped off of God's radar. It also seemed to be more prevalent to me now that I didn't have a church family for the first time in my life.

It had been almost a year since I moved back home and though I was leaning towards joining a church again, I still

> *Hello God, I'm still here!*

wanted to keep my distance. Prior to Sista passing away, I considered joining the church she and her family were members of. I downloaded the membership form from their website and signed up for volunteer opportunities. Being a member at a large church would allow me to be a church member and only be as involved as I desired. Coming from a small church and being there from the beginning required a lot of involvement and because of the way things ended, I was determined I was not doing that again.

After Sista passed, attending the church she was a member of wasn't the same. It was difficult being in service and not seeing her on the choir or having her beside me during Bible study. I attended only a few services there after she passed. I had never completed and returned the membership form, so I decided to continue to visit other churches. I began to regularly attend Christ Revealed Church (CRC) and started to feel very strongly that this was the place I needed to join.

This was not what I desired! Yes, I was attending regularly and thoroughly enjoying the teaching, but it felt a little more comfortable than I desired. I know that sounds strange, but I didn't want to end up overly involved in church again. CRC felt like one big happy family, and I feared being connected to a church family again. Though it was a much larger congregation than I had been a part of at God's Grace International (GGI), it was smaller than the church my sister attended. With that being the case, I knew I wouldn't be able to hide very long.

The most I wanted to do at this time was be a church member. Let me have my name on the roll and I'm good with that. During my time at Leading Ladies Ministry (LLM), I worked with teen girls and young adult ladies and I wrote a booklet on purity for that target audience. I felt as though God wanted me to continue that work so I picked back up a blog that I began working on a few years back. I believed that if I shared information from the booklet in my blog entries it would satisfy what God was requiring of me.

After working on the blog again, I still felt I needed to join CRC. Even with strong feelings about joining, I continued to fight. I wanted to find something in the church structure at CRC that too closely resembled my previous experience and that would be my reason for not joining.

I requested a meeting with Pastor and First Lady Young to ask questions about the organizational structure of CRC. I was certain that I would hear something that would cosign my fight against joining this church. The meeting was on a Tuesday afternoon. Pastor Young liked to use the sanctuary as his work and meeting space, so he had a table set up in the pulpit that he worked from. I sat down at the table across from the two of them and begin to pose my questions. He answered each one, and none of his responses gave me a reason to run.

God then decides to turn the table on me. Pastor Young looks at me and says, *"I'm not saying I'm being prophetic, but I see you working with young ladies and teaching them about life, purpose and purity."* As he was talking, he drew a diagram depicting what God was saying. Life was the core element with purpose and purity branching off. There was a third branch to be filled in. Though my initial response was to shake my head in disbelief, I spoke up and told him that the third branch is love.

Well! This was definitely not what I was expecting. I had never spoken with Pastor or First Lady Young about what

God had told me to do, so I knew that this was God getting my attention. At the conclusion of the meeting, I asked for a membership card and became a member of CRC that day.

It's amazing how an act of obedience can immediately release other information. I joined CRC on Tuesday and the Saturday that followed was the day for the monthly leadership meeting for members of CRC. I attended the meeting, and felt compelled to ask Kari if she wanted to go to lunch afterwards. Kari was one of the newer members who I made acquaintance with since visiting CRC. She and I would chat regularly after services. She wasn't available immediately after the meeting, but we met up about an hour later for lunch.

In our chats after church, I had mentioned to her some of what I experienced at GGI, but had not gone into any great detail with her. When we met for lunch, we met at a shopping center because we were undecided on where we wanted to go. I agreed to drive, so she got in my car and we decided where we would eat. As we headed to the restaurant, I'm not sure why I asked, but I asked her where she was from again. She confirmed that she was from Saluda, SC.

I then asked, *"Do you know any Wilcoxs (pronounced wil-cōh) from Saluda?"*

She responded, *"No, I know some Wilcoxs (pronounced wil-cŏx)."*

I then said, *"Oh, that's ok then. The bishop I mentioned to you from my previous church is from Saluda, but his last name is Wilcox (pronounced wil-cōh)."*

She then exclaimed as she almost flipped out the car, *"Oh my God! I know exactly who you're talking about!"*

I'm completely shocked and I respond, *"Are you serious?"*

She says, *"Yes! He has been a lying, manipulator all of his life!"*

She described him to confirm we were talking about the same person

At that point, I really could not believe what I was hearing. *He changed* Not only did she personally know him, they have some *the pronunc* shared relatives and she knew much of his family history. *of his last* Not to my surprise, much of what he had presented to us *name* were lies as I suspected. Though I was relieved to finally *but still* know the truth, it was disheartening to consider all of the *spelled it* relationships that Pastor Dowdy severed as a result of her *the same.* relationship with him. On the other hand, I knew that God was up to something to bring this to light less than a week after I joined CRC.

> **He is touched by what concerns us**

God never ceases to amaze me. God's care for us is unparalleled and He is touched by what concerns us, and having the truth revealed to me allowed me to see that. After learning this information about Bishop Wilcox, I didn't want to run to Pastor Dowdy or the members of GGI to share or have an "I told you so" moment. Honestly my heart still hurt for them and what they were subjected to at the hands of Bishop Wilcox.

Once I was released from GGI, it was no longer a priority for me to prove anything about Bishop Wilcox. It really never should have been a priority. It's challenging to trust God when we think we know what's best. I've learned that reclining in trusting Him is the best position to be in.

LIFE Expression:
Find contentment in trusting God.
He leaves nothing undone.

PAUSE & REFLECT. PRAY & LISTEN.

◆

Consider a time when truth was revealed to you after a relationship. What was your response and how did you handle the truth?

_____

_____

_____

_____

_____

_____

_____

_____

_____

_____

_____

_____

_____

_____

_____

"If possible, so far as it depends on you, be at peace with all men."
Romans 12:18

$\blacklozenge \quad \blacklozenge \quad \blacklozenge$

FORGED FORGIVENESS

If reconciliation on any level is going to happen, true forgiveness can't be forced. Effort is required from all involved parties. The heart that gives the apology must be ready to move forward and the heart that receives the apology must be ready to move forward. It's beautiful that God truly knows the heart of man. He prepares us and presents opportunities for us to show forth His glory in relationships.

> *True forgiveness can't be forced*

Wednesday, May 16, 2012, I had the unexpected thought, *It's my anniversary, I need to call April and remind her*. It was two years ago on this day when I was "released" from God's Grace International (GGI). I chuckled at the thought, but didn't make the call to April. Christ Revealed Church (CRC) holds Bible study on Wednesday nights, and during this time our classes were separate studies for men and women. The women's class was reading the book, *So Long Insecurity* by Beth Moore. This particular evening, the minister that taught shared about how she had to forgive her parents for the things they did that without their knowledge caused her some emotional damage. Other ladies in the class also shared similar stories. While they were sharing, I thought,

Well, since both of my parents are deceased this isn't any thing I'll have to do.

The women's class met downstairs in the church and cell phone reception was very poor in that area. When I left church that evening, I had a message from my friend Sarah. She attends GGI and after my release, she and I maintained our friendship. When I returned her call, she wanted me to know that Pastor Dowdy had been asking about me, and she suggested that I give her a call. I let her know that Pastor Dowdy was open to call me if she was concerned about how I was doing. When the call ended, I called the minister that was over the women's ministry at CRC and shared the conversation with her. In an honest expression I told her, *"I feel some type of way about this."*

She responded, *"I feel some type of way too!"* After we both laughed about our responses, she said *"You know, you may have to go ahead and make that phone call."* I was still not feeling it, so I responded, *"Hmm... Ok. I'll have to pray about it."*

My resistance to contact Pastor Dowdy didn't just come from that moment. There was history to my hesitation. A few months after I moved back to Greenville, I made attempts to reach out to her. I would pray for her when she crossed my mind. After praying for her one day, I felt impressed to send her a financial gift, so I did. After some time passed, the check had not cleared my account so I contacted Sarah and requested that she ask Pastor Dowdy if she received the check. She informed Sarah that she received it and shredded it. Her desire was that I stop trying to reach out to her. I took the cue and did just that. I ceased all attempts to communicate. My only hope beyond that was that if our paths crossed we would at least be cordial.

When my sister passed away, I didn't receive any condolences from Pastor Dowdy or GGI. I honestly felt embarrassed sitting at the funeral knowing I had served with this congregation for ten years and there was no acknowledgements from them while cards and flowers were sent from other churches I associated with while I was at GGI. If that wasn't bad enough, I received word that church members were discouraged to reach out to me and that Pastor Dowdy said she didn't know I had a sister. I suppose she forgot the time they spent together in the waiting room while I was in surgery the previous year.

Lord, give me an opportunity to show love including Pastor Carbm.

Hearing this brought no comfort as I'm sure it wasn't designed to. I couldn't understand where this degree of disdain towards me was coming from. By now, the magnitude of devastation from my sister's death was overwhelming and I didn't have the strength to reciprocate those feelings. While riding in the funeral car leaving the gravesite from Sista's funeral, I silently prayed, *Lord, give me an opportunity to show love.*

The next day, I found out Pastor Dowdy had gotten married. Yes, the very next day after Sista's funeral. I remember thinking, *Ok God, I want to show love, but couldn't You have given me a little time?* Lol! I thought it was a rumor initially but it was verified as truth a few days later. I didn't act immediately. I waited about a month and sent a congratulations card and financial gift to Pastor Dowdy. This time the check cleared and a generic thank you card followed a few weeks later. I had no expectations beyond that, but was relieved that at least it was a cordial exchange between us.

Based on those incidents, I didn't feel a wide open welcome door to reach out to her. However, I did pray about it. After praying about it, I felt that I should call. Knowing me, I knew that if I didn't move on it right away, I would not do it. I called Pastor Dowdy the day after Sarah reached out to me. After several rings, her voice mail picked up and her mailbox was full so I could not leave a message. I thought, *Well ok God, I tried.* God evidently had other plans and was not done making them plain to me.

The following weekend was Memorial Day weekend. CRC hosted a church trip to a theme park in a neighboring state. I participated in the trip that year. Part of the reason for the trip was to attend the annual Memorial Day weekend Gospel concert at this theme park. So after a few hours of riding, we settled in to the amphitheater for the concert. There are thousands of people at the theme park on this particular Saturday, and several hundred of them attend this concert. The seat I was in was the first row of the walkway in the middle of the amphitheater. A few hours into the concert, I was standing enjoying the performances. While I was standing, I looked to the left and Minister Loman was coming down the walkway. I had not seen or spoken with her since I left her home after surgery in May 2010.

Without even thinking about it, I found myself stepping forward into her path to speak. It was like my

> *God was trying to get my attention*

body moved without my full permission. I greeted her, and during our exchange, she brings up Pastor Dowdy. She expressed excitement about Pastor Dowdy's husband and makes the remark that I really should meet him. My response was, *"Oh, ok,"* as I'm thinking, *Is she serious?* Pastor Dowdy and I hadn't verbally spoken in two years, so meeting her husband wasn't on my agenda.

As I mentioned in an earlier chapter, most of the relationships I had with people at GGI had ended. So running in to Minister Loman at a theme park in another state and having a pleasant exchange with her was a shock. I could not deny that God was trying to get my attention. In the weeks that followed that exchange, I was feeling I needed to attempt to call Pastor Dowdy again.

I am still not understanding what God is wanting from me, so I begin to question Him. *"Didn't I try already, God?"* Some relationships will never be the same after drastic changes. I knew I was not the same person and I didn't assume that she was either. The thought of restoration of that relationship shook me because I couldn't see it beyond what it once was. While restoration is not the usual outcome of severed relationships, as Christians we should desire reconciliation. After looking closer at the meanings of these words, it made much more sense to me.

> **restore**: *to put back to a former place, or to a former position, rank, etc.*

> **reconcile**: *to win over to friendliness; cause to become amicable; to compose or settle (a quarrel, dispute, etc.); to bring into agreement or harmony; make compatible or consistent:*

As I'm pondering these thoughts one day, and feeling strongly about calling, I received an e-mail from a company that I train for periodically. The e-mail was for an assignment to teach some classes in the same city as GGI. I was excited about the opportunity and the extra money. I still hadn't made the call to Pastor Dowdy and was still questioning it. Just moments later, I received another e-mail saying the client was postponing so the assignment was cancelled until further notice. I responded requesting that they keep me posted on the status.

I then decided to finally make another attempt to call Pastor Dowdy. Again, there was no answer, but the voice mail wasn't full this time. I left a message and was content at feeling I had done what God wanted me to do. In a matter of minutes, I received a phone call that the training assignment was back on. I thought, *God, you really have a sense of humor.* Though in the natural, these two contacts didn't have any connection other than location, it was more than a coincidence that the assignment was postponed then suddenly available again once I moved forward and obeyed God. Following instructions through the process is required in order to progress.

From that last contact, it was several weeks before I received a response from Pastor Dowdy. I knew she didn't regularly check her voice messages so the time lapse wasn't a surprise. She called while I was in a training class, but she left a voice message. The message was very generic and didn't leave the impression that she had been asking about me as Sarah said. I wondered if I should have never reached out although I know what I felt and I could not ignore the obvious signs that pointed towards her.

About a week later, I received another call from her. This time I was available to answer. After all the attempts leading up to this moment, I was still shocked that this conversation was happening. Bishop Wilcox was no longer a part of her life, and unfortunately none of his promises ever came to fruition. The conversation was brief, but left a great impression. There were explanations and apologies that I had not anticipated, yet I was so grateful for this moment.

The following month, Pastor Dowdy was celebrating a milestone birthday and it happened to fall on a Sunday that year. I contacted Sarah to let her know I was coming to service that Sunday to surprise Pastor Dowdy. When she saw me, she was not only surprised, but she was moved to tears. I believe that we should still be able to show love and kindness towards others even when relationships take unexpected turns. We still get to choose how we act and respond.

I've shared many more pleasant moments and conversations beyond that one with Pastor Dowdy. We are both in different places in life now, so the relationship is different, but it's a genuine reconnection. As with all relationships, it takes effort from both parties to remain connected. I know that all relationships don't experience reconciliation, and I reached a point where I did not think this one would. God has the final say and for that I'm humbled and glad.

LIFE Expression:
The strength of a relationship is not found in what comes to test it, but it's found in what it overcomes.

PAUSE & REFLECT. PRAY & LISTEN.

When have you had to pursue reconciliation and forgiveness in a relationship even though you didn't think you should? Do you have severed relationships that you feel the need to reconcile with the person?

_____

_____

_____

_____

_____

_____

_____

_____

_____

_____

_____

_____

_____

_____

_____

_____

"Listen carefully: Unless a grain of wheat is buried in the ground, dead to the world, it is never any more than a grain of wheat. But if it is buried, it sprouts and reproduces itself many times over. In the same way, anyone who holds on to life just as it is destroys that life. But if you let it go, reckless in your love, you'll have it forever, real and eternal."
John 12: 24,25 MSG

RELEASED TO BLOOM

I've shared some intimate moments in the previous chapters with hopes that you would see some parallels in your own life. Though your personal events may differ from mine, we all face things that come to halt us from progressing. I shared abbreviated versions of pivotal moments to convey to you that we are designed to connect and progress.

One or even a few bad experiences should not keep you out of relationships, church or any community that can add strength to your life. We all experience emotional pain though we all respond to it differently. Pain can push you towards faith or make you cower in fear. It's interesting how in some ways we quarantine an entire organization or group based on a bad experience. We tend to only do that in certain areas of our lives.

People deal with bad employers, companies and bosses daily, but they don't keep themselves out of the workforce. Athletes get injured and return to their sport. Chefs return to the kitchen after being cut. Drivers and passengers continue to commute after being involved in accidents. There is a larger focus or goal that pushes them to try again.

It reminds me of how as children we are admonished not to touch the stove and to steer clear of sharp objects such as knives and scissors. If you have small children, you have to child proof your home to keep them away from certain items and places. The ban is only temporary. Once children learn the appropriate use of places and items that they were previously restricted from, they have full access and use while heeding the needed warnings and precautions.

Take the child that may have been burned by the stove, cut by scissors, fallen down the stairs, or experienced any event that left a bad memory and possibly a scar; they suffered an injury as a result of not following instructions or not having the *right* instructions. Though they may steer clear of these items for a while, they eventually realize they can use them, but must use them correctly. We don't always arrive at moments with all the knowledge we need to handle ourselves or others appropriately, so we obtain injuries. That's not a permanent stop light, it's simply a lesson from that moment.

Sometimes being able to move forward requires us to look back. My process required me to reconnect to what hurt me. Like many others, I experienced conflict and challenges in relationships and church. Attacks come to separate us from things we need the most. We need relationships and we need community. It seems that when we experience hurts in these areas, they send us in a shell where we move forward with extreme caution if we move forward at all.

After my initial meeting with Pastor and Lady Young in September 2011, I was faced with deciding between faith and fear. I was certain about my desire to help young adult ladies and grateful that God confirmed it through Pastor Young. Young adults make so many life altering decisions without the needed wisdom and guidance. My desire to help young adult ladies came from all the times I and so many others have said, "If I knew then, what I know now." If I can be an agent to ensure that they know better, I can also encourage them to do better.

Once I was clear on my why, I continued to talk to God about what to do. Knowing why but not what led to moments of frustration. After experiencing pain and loss we want to be exempt from doing what is required from us. I often thought, *God, do I have to deal with the potential of more loss and rejection?* Wanting to obey God, I wrestled with the sting of wounds that were still healing. I also didn't have a clear plan on how to implement what God wanted me to do.

During the time that I was praying for what to do next was when God had me reconcile relationships and reconnect to a place I associated with pain. I've shared much of that time in the previous pages including my reluctance during those times. While having to walk through that process and still uncertain about what was ahead, I wanted to retreat and back completely away from the instructions. I remember hearing one day, *You can do things your way and enjoy the fruit of your labor or obey what I have told you and enjoy the fruit of my promises.* Another audible interruption of my thoughts, so I knew God was again speaking to me. That was enough for me to keep pressing forward.

I had to trust that God would continue to carry me the way He always has. After continued prayer and planning, the answer resulted in a nonprofit organization where we are able to share vital information and provide resources for a number of young adult ladies. This was never on my agenda. God's plan for us is bigger than our own desires. Giving God a "Yes" does not exempt you or place you in a bubble. This process is not easy. I have thoughts of quitting, but I know that my heart would be miserable outside of my calling. When I'm feeling this way, there usually is a call, text or conversation with a young lady that refocuses me on my why and reminds me of the bigger picture.

Even with the wonderful things that have blossomed from ugly places, I still deal with the emotional residue. I miss my mother and my sister daily. I still suffer pain and loss in relationships that I thought were forever. I'm not immune from any of the difficulties that come with living and loving. I welcome where I am with no regrets about where I've been and what I've experienced. Through separation, unbearable loss and many new beginnings, I have a peace in knowing that God is for me. As confident as we may be in our now, there will always be uncertainties about the future. I choose to continue to take risks in life and in love because God's consistency overshadows all uncertainties.

I learned one of the greatest lessons this year through nature. I moved into a rental property in February 2013. Later in the year, I noticed a single rose that would bloom on the rose bush behind the shrubbery out front. The results were the same for the next two years. In 2014 and 2015 the bush produced one rose. In June 2016 I looked at the bush and noticed eleven roses in full bloom on the bush. I snapped a picture to capture the beauty, but I also paused to reflect on what I was seeing.

Over the years, I had not tended to this rose bush in any manner. I would only take note of the fruit I saw on it. There were times when it looked as if it may have died, and I didn't do anything to try to save it. I would just wait and see what and if it produced. You see, I didn't plant the rose bush and don't know who did. It was there when I moved in. Honestly, I didn't even know it existed until I saw the rose it produced.

Evidently, it didn't need me to tend to it. Even in times when it looked as if it was dead or dying, it still produced at least one rose. Then this year when it still appeared that it may have died, it produced eleven roses. Seeing those roses encouraged me. Weather may not have always been favorable, but without fail, the rose bush got what it needed to produce and multiply. I believe that no matter the circumstances surrounding me, God decides.

So it is with our lives. We look as if it's over many times. Those around us don't know what to do to help. Your life is in the hands of the ultimate care giver. Every experience up to this point and even those to come are preparation for you to bloom. There is an expectation for that which is planted to produce fruit. There is a seed of righteousness in you and there is a need for the fruit from that seed.

I had to push past the temptation to remain a bud and push to blossom. Not just for me, but for every life that is dependent upon mine. I admonish you to do the same. There is great freedom in following God's plan for your life. Your life is unfolding into a beautiful story. ALL THINGS are working for your good. Take the lesson from every moment. Life Speaks!

LIFE Expression:

In life, we experience moments that take our breath away and we feel elated. Then there are moments that knock the wind out of us and we feel deflated. At the end of each moment, you are still breathing.
Inhale. Exhale. Continue to LIVE!

PAUSE & REFLECT. PRAY & LISTEN.

◆

What lessons have you gained from your life experiences?

_____

_____

_____

_____

_____

_____

_____

_____

_____

_____

_____

_____

_____

_____

_____

_____

ABOUT THE AUTHOR

As an advocate of love and life, Tammy Carpenter firmly believes that love covers a multitude of sin and that we are to have an abundant life as God has promised. While she enjoys her career as a Software Consultant, Tammy's passion is to see young women live the full, abundant life that God has purposed for them.

Tammy merged her passion for helping young adult women with lessons from her life and personal experiences and founded enLife in 2013. enLife is a nonprofit, 501(c)3 organization with a focus on building and impacting the lives of young adult women. enLife offers programs and resources to help young women succeed through life transitions. Tammy proudly serves as the Executive Director of enLife and has the pleasure of mentoring and encouraging many young women.

Tammy is a native of and resides in Greenville, South Carolina. For over 20 years, Tammy has served in various capacities in ministry including Youth/Young Adult Ministry, Women's Ministry and Administration. She is a member of Changing Your Mind Ministries (CYMM) in Greenville, SC under the leadership of Pastor Wendell & Lady Nita Jones. Tammy was recently licensed as a Minister at CYMM and serves on their Ministerial Staff.